Home Soap Making

Easy Ideas for Making and Gifting Scented Suds

Kimberly Layton

LEISURE ARTS, INC. • Maumelle, Arkansas

Introduction

Create beautiful handmade soaps that are perfect for gift giving! You'll find easy instructions for 13 types of soap that can all be made in minutes. Make a batch of Coffee Latte Soap for your friends or create a wedding favor with Botanical Soap Sticks. Soap is the perfect handmade gift for any occasion!

Handmade
just for you

Contents

Getting Started

Soap making does not have to be complicated, especially when you take advantage of the wide variety of ready-made soap bases that are available. These bases are ready to use immediately, so you can focus your creativity on the colors, fragrances, and additives you'd like to include in your recipes. With just a handful of ingredients and basic kitchen supplies, you can craft beautiful handmade soaps in minutes.

SOAP BASES

All of the projects in this book use melt and pour soap bases. They're convenient, easy to use, and will allow you to create beautiful soaps in no time. You'll find a wide variety of soap bases at your local craft store. You can change the soap base in most soap projects to suit your taste—some of the projects even use multiple soap bases. Try a few different bases, and you'll quickly find a favorite. Here are a few of my go-tos.

SOAP BASE	BENEFITS
Clear glycerin	Great lather
Goat's milk	Available in a suspension formula that works well for incorporating natural additives
Shea butter	Great for your skin, available in a suspension formula for special projects
Coconut milk	Light smell, feels great on your skin

NATURAL ADDITIVES

Many natural additives, like dried botanicals, can be incorporated in your soap recipes to enhance the texture or style of the finished product. Many of them can act as gentle exfoliants in most soaps. Use your additives to form a layer on the top or bottom of your soap, or suspend them evenly throughout the soap. My favorite natural additives include:

- Dried lavender
- Poppy seeds
- Pink Himalayan salt
- Loofah sponges
- Activated charcoal
- Lemon peel
- Coconut
- Green tea

MOLDS

You probably have a few items on hand that can be used as soap molds. Anything from an ice cube tray to a paper cup will do, but there are a few options that work best.

Silicone molds: These are my favorite! They are easy to use, especially when it comes to removing the finished soap, and come in a million styles. You can also use silicone ice cube trays.

Plastic soap molds: These work well and they're inexpensive.

Loaf molds: These are available in silicone, wood, and hard plastic with removable sides.

MOLD RELEASES

I don't use mold releases for my projects, but they can be helpful, especially if you're using a plastic mold. Add a light layer of petroleum jelly or vegetable oil to the mold before pouring the soap. Use caution—it's possible the mold release will discolor your soap. It's best to test a mold release before making a large batch of soap.

FRAGRANCES & ESSENTIAL OILS

You can find a wide variety of soap fragrances and essential oils at your local craft store. High-quality essential oils are my favorite to use because of their aromatherapy benefits.

SOAP COLORANTS

There are loads of options for coloring your soap creations. You can use cosmetic-grade colorants, mica powders, ground spices, cocoa powder, coffee, or solid soap base colorants that melt. For most of the projects in this book, I used liquid cosmetic-grade colorants to color the soap. These come in a multitude of colors, so it's easy to find the perfect shade. Do not use regular food coloring in your soap—it is not likely to blend into the soap mixture.

RUBBING ALCOHOL

Have a small spray bottle filled with rubbing alcohol on hand for any soap project. Once you've finished pouring your soap, lightly spray it with the alcohol, and you will see any bubbles disappear!

Basic Steps for Soap Making

Follow these basic steps for any project in this book. Here, I'm making about a cup of soap, but I usually make two to three cups at once using a large glass measuring cup for easy pouring.

1 Cut the soap base into small squares and add them to a microwave-safe container. I melt the soap in the microwave, but you can also use a double boiler on the stovetop if you prefer.

2 Microwave the soap on high for 30 seconds, then stir well. Repeat once more.

3 If the soap is not yet fully melted, heat it for an additional 20–30 seconds at a time, stirring after each interval. The soap pieces melt quite a bit while you're stirring, so make sure you stir thoroughly before heating again. It's best to heat the soap as little as possible to keep it from boiling.

4 Once the soap base is completely melted, add your desired fragrance, essential oils, coloring, and additives, and stir well.

5 Quickly pour the soap into a mold. Let it cool completely before removing it. It should pop out easily.

Tips & Tricks

- If the soap starts to set before you pour it, simply reheat it for a few seconds.
- Melt a bit of extra soap, because some will stick to the sides of the container as you pour it.
- Always make sure your soap is completely melted before pouring. This will prevent splashes of hot soap and give your finished soap an even color.
- Keep a silicone ice cube tray on hand and pour any excess soap into it. In addition to the project you're making, you'll have cute mini soaps, and you won't waste a drop of your beautiful soap mixture.
- You can place soap molds in the refrigerator to help the soap cool and set, but this can cause condensation to form on your soap.
- To release soap from a plastic mold, firmly press on one small spot on the mold and wait for the soap to start to release from the mold. It will pop out once the suction is released.
- Do not wash your soap making supplies in the dishwasher.
- I like to let my soap set for 24 hours before packaging it. This gives the soap a chance to become nice and firm.
- If you'd like to make a large batch of soap, simply double or triple the recipes in this book. Doubling recipes saves time, and you'll get twice the amount of soap for the same amount of effort as a single batch.
- To determine how much soap you need for any mold, use a measuring cup to pour water into the mold. Note how much water the mold holds. You'll need to melt the same amount of soap, plus a little extra to account for some of the soap sticking to the sides of the container during pouring.

The Projects

Now that you know a bit about the supplies you'll need and the basic steps for soap making, it's time to pick a project and start creating. These recipes allow you to take a handful of ingredients and make lovely creations for you, your family, and your friends in just a few minutes. There are a range of styles and ideas so you can build your skills with each project and learn which ingredients and techniques you like best. You'll find miniature soaps, rustic designs, and classic concoctions that take advantage of the benefits of natural botanicals and essential oils. As you begin to feel confident with the process, try experimenting to make these recipes your own. Substitute your favorite soap bases, colors, essential oils, and fragrances to match your personal tastes and preferences. Use the plants you may already have growing in your garden in a totally new way by drying and adding them to your recipes. There are endless opportunities for creativity. In addition to the recipes, you'll find ideas for packaging each project for gifting. I had so much fun creating these recipes, and I hope you have just as much fun making them!

♡ you

charcoal
SOAP

Grapefruit Pink Himalayan Salt Soap

MAKES 2 BARS

Why not give your feet an extra special treat with this exfoliating soap? The coarse salt will help smooth away rough patches, while the rich goat's milk will soften and moisturize. The invigorating scent of the grapefruit essential oil can help freshen feet and is also known to help reduce headaches and mental fatigue. The salt has a natural pink color that makes these soaps a beautiful addition to any bathroom.

Shopping List

- 1½ cups goat's milk soap base
- ½ cup coarse pink Himalayan salt
- 5–6 drops grapefruit essential oil
- Two 3"-diameter silicone tart molds
- Rubbing alcohol in small spray bottle
- Microwave-safe container
- Wooden stir stick

Sea Salt Detox

Pink Himalayan sea salt is packed with minerals that can help detoxify skin by drawing out heavy metals, dirt, and bacteria from pores. It's also a natural deodorizer.

MAKE IT! • GRAPEFRUIT PINK HIMALAYAN SALT SOAP

1 Prepare the molds by adding a layer of pink Himalayan salt to the bottom of each mold.

2 Melt the goat's milk soap base.

3 Add the grapefruit essential oil. Stir well and gently pour the soap into the molds.

4 Lightly spray the surface of the soap with the rubbing alcohol to remove bubbles.

5 Let the soap set until firm and remove from the molds.

6 After removing the soap from the molds, you can press any extra salt on the top, if desired.

Package each soap in a pie or tart box. Secure the lid with decorative string like baker's twine. For an extra special touch, add a paper flower that complements the color of the Himalayan salt and a tag.

Milk & Honey Soap

MAKES 3 BARS

Milk and honey are a classic combination for any skin product, offering numerous healing and moisturizing properties. Along with these benefits, this soap has a lovely, simple scent. Try adding your favorite essential oil to create the perfect go-to soap for your daily routine.

Shopping List

- ½ cup honey soap base
- 1 cup goat's milk soap base
- 6–8 drops buttermilk fragrance
- Three 2½" x 3½" honeycomb soap molds
- Rubbing alcohol in small spray bottle
- 2 microwave-safe containers
- Wooden stir stick

Simply Honey

Honey is known for its ability to moisturize and repair skin. It's wonderfully soothing, making it the perfect ingredient to relive dry or irritated skin.

MAKE IT! • MILK & HONEY SOAP

1 Melt the honey soap base.

2 Add 3–4 drops of the buttermilk fragrance. Mix well and pour the soap into the molds, filling each one halfway. Lightly spray the surface of the soap with the rubbing alcohol to remove bubbles. Let the soap set for 20–30 minutes.

3 Melt the goat's milk soap base. Add 3–4 drops of the buttermilk fragrance and stir well. To help the two soap layers stick together, lightly spray the surface of the soap in the molds again with rubbing alcohol. Pour the goat's milk soap into the molds. Lightly spray the surface with the rubbing alcohol to remove bubbles. Let set and remove from the molds.

Nourishing Goat's Milk

Goat's milk is filled with vitamins and minerals that help nourish the skin, especially Vitamin A. The lactic acid in the goat's milk helps gently wash away dead skin cells to leave skin smooth and soft.

Pair this soap with a wooden soap dish. Use stamps to create a label. Secure the soap on top of the soap dish with twine and attach the label.

Mint Leaves

MAKES 10 LEAF SOAPS

Sometimes we could all use an extra pick-me-up in the morning. This soap is the perfect way to start your day. The glycerin base produces a full, luxurious lather, while the spearmint essential oil causes a cool tingle on your skin and gives off an invigorating scent—just what you need to kickstart your daily routine. For an extra special touch, use a suspension formula and add dried mint leaves to the soap. These soap leaves look beautiful displayed in a dish in your bathroom, or you can package them in a sheer bag as a refreshing gift.

SHOPPING LIST

- 1½ cups clear glycerin soap base
- 2 shades green soap coloring
- 7–10 drops spearmint essential oil
- 10-leaf soap mold (mine is 10" x 5")
- Rubbing alcohol in small spray bottle
- Microwave-safe container
- Wooden stir stick

Marvelous Mint

In addition to adding a refreshing scent and a cooling tingle to your soap, spearmint essential oil contains vitamins that can help condition your skin. It's particularly good at protecting dry or chapped skin.

MAKE IT! • MINT LEAVES

1 Melt the glycerin soap base.

2 Add the spearmint essential oil and 3–5 drops of the lighter green soap coloring. Stir well and pour into a few of the leaves in the mold.

3 Add 3–5 drops of the darker green soap coloring. Stir well and pour into a few of the leaves in the mold.

4 Add a few more drops of the darker green soap coloring. Stir well and pour into the remaining leaves in the mold.

5 Lightly spray the surface of the soap with the rubbing alcohol to remove bubbles. Let the soap set until firm and remove from the mold.

Fill a small flower pot with crinkle-cut paper and nestle a few of the soap leaves on top. Finish off the look with matching ribbon and you'll have an adorable decoration for any bathroom.

Mini Spa Travel Soap

MAKES 3 TRAVEL-SIZE SOAPS

Both rosemary and eucalyptus essential oils are natural deodorizers and help fight bacteria, making them excellent soap ingredients. These soaps are perfectly sized to be packaged in tins for traveling, or you can make an entire batch to keep on hand in your bathroom at home. Their soothing scent is wonderfully relaxing to help you unwind after a long day, whether you've been on the road or working around the house.

Shopping List

- ¾–1 cup white glycerin soap base
- 2 drops eucalyptus essential oil
- 2 drops rosemary essential oil
- Standard silicone cupcake mold
- 3"-diameter metal tin with lid
- Wax paper
- Rubbing alcohol in small spray bottle
- Microwave-safe container
- Wooden stir stick

Renewing Rosemary

Rosemary is said to help improve memory. In fact, Greek scholars wore rosemary when taking exams to help improve performance. It is also a natural pain reliever, helping to soothe tired muscles and joints.

MAKE IT! • MINI SPA TRAVEL SOAP

1 Melt the glycerin soap base. Add the essential oils and stir well. Pour into the mold, filling each space with about ½" of soap. Lightly spray the surface of the soap with the rubbing alcohol to remove bubbles. Let the soap set until firm and remove from the mold.

2 Using the base of the soap as a guide, cut a circle of wax paper for each piece of soap.

3 Place a wax paper circle in the bottom of the tin. Stack the soaps in the tin, placing a wax paper circle between each one.

Relaxing Eucalyptus

Eucalyptus essential oil shares many of the same benefits of rosemary essential oil. It is a natural deodorizer, antibacterial, and anti-inflammatory, making it wonderful for use on sore muscles. The scent is also incredibly relaxing and calming.

Package two to three soaps in a circular tin, placing pieces of wax paper between each one. Use stamps to create a label for the tin and attach it to the lid, using glue if necessary.

Gemstone Soap

MAKES 6 SOAPS

Combining a glycerin and an olive oil soap base produces wonderful results. You get to take advantage of the hydrating and skin-conditioning properties of the olive oil, as well as the rich lather of the glycerin. Have fun creating variations of this soap by adding the mica powder to both of your soap mixtures, or by adding a touch of mica powder to the mixture between pouring the soap. Use your creativity!

Shopping List

- 1½ cups white glycerin soap base
- 1 cup olive oil soap base
- 10 drops lemongrass essential oil
- ½ teaspoon pink mica powder
- 2 shades pink soap coloring
- 6-square soap mold (mine is 4" x 6")
- Rubbing alcohol in small spray bottle
- 2 microwave-safe containers
- Wooden stir stick
- Sharp knife or flat metal soap slicer
- Small bowl

Energizing Lemongrass

Lemongrass essential oil helps to boost energy and can also alleviate muscle pain, making it perfect for the start of your day. Lemongrass is also wonderful for your skin, helping to cleanse and heal.

MAKE IT! • GEMSTONE SOAP

1 Mix the mica powder and ½ teaspoon of alcohol together in a small bowl. Stir well to remove any clumps from the mica powder.

2 Melt the glycerin soap base and olive oil soap base in separate bowls. Add 5 drops of essential oil to each soap mixture. Add the mica mixture and a few drops of the first shade of pink coloring to the glycerin soap and stir well. Add a few drops of the second shade of pink coloring to the olive oil soap and stir well.

3 Pour the soap mixtures into the mold, alternating between the two to create a blend of the soaps.

4 Lightly spray the surface of the soap with the rubbing alcohol to remove bubbles. Let the soap set until firm and remove from the mold.

5 Use a sharp knife or metal soap slicer to make 6–10 slices on each soap square, creating a gemstone look.

Add a few soaps to a small jar—a shiny lid pairs wonderfully with the gemstone look. Create a label and attach it to the jar lid. For a decorative touch, tie a ribbon around the outside of the lid.

Botanical Soap Sticks

MAKES 7–8 STICKS PER RECIPE

Creating soap sticks allows you to put together a lovely package that samples a range of recipes. These three recipes use different natural ingredients, each with their own benefits, so you'll always have exactly what you need on hand. The marigold recipe combines anti-inflammatory marigolds with stress-relieving bergamot, perfect for soothing irritated skin. The lavender recipe is relaxing and calming, wonderful to enjoy at the end of a long day. The lemon poppy seed recipe is invigorating and exfoliating, a refreshing pick-me-up for your morning. Enjoy each one when you need it!

Shopping List

FOR ALL VARIETIES

- 6 cups goat's milk soap base (2 cups for each recipe)
- 5" x 16" loaf soap mold
- Rubbing alcohol in small spray bottle
- Microwave-safe container
- Wooden stir stick
- Colored tape
- Flat metal soap slicer
- Sharp knife or stick

Shopping List

MARIGOLD SOAP STICKS

- 10 drops bergamot essential oil
- 5 drops green soap coloring
- ¼ cup dried marigold

LAVENDER SOAP STICKS

- 10 drops lavender essential oil
- 1 teaspoon dried lavender

LEMON POPPY SEED SOAP STICKS

- 10 drops lemon essential oil
- 6–7 drops yellow soap coloring
- 1 teaspoon poppy seeds

Bergamot Boost

Bergamot essential oil is known to help reduce stress, boost energy, and create an overall feeling of cheerfulness. When applied to the skin as in soap, it can help to reduce the appearance of scars and soothe irritated skin.

1 Melt 2 cups of the goat's milk soap base. Add the essential oil and soap coloring for the marigold soap stick recipe. Mix well and pour into the mold. Mark the height of the soap with a small piece of colored tape.

2 Sprinkle the dried marigolds evenly across the top of the soap and poke them into the soap randomly with a sharp knife or stick. This will secure some of the dried marigolds in the soap. Lightly spray the surface of the soap with the rubbing alcohol to remove bubbles.

3 Let the soap set until firm, then remove from the mold and slice into sticks using a basic metal soap slicer for best results. Repeat Steps 1–3 with the ingredients for the lavender and lemon poppy seed recipes, using the colored tape in Step 1 to pour the soap to the same depth each time.

Dynamic Duo

Poppy seeds contain a high amount of linolenic acid, which can help maintain a healthy complexion. But the combination of poppy seed and lemon can do even more. Lemon and poppy seeds are a wonderful way to treat skin inflammation. Used together, they can help alleviate redness and itchiness and soothe burns.

Create gift bags by placing one of each soap stick in a drawstring bag. Use stamps to create labels for the bags, or you can hand letter them. Use the strings on the bags to attach the labels.

Charcoal Cleansing Bar

MAKES 3 BARS

Charcoal works to detoxify your skin without dehydrating it, making it a wonderful face and body cleanser. This soap is a great way to prevent blemishes as it helps remove excess oil and also polishes skin with gentle exfoliation. Keep several of these bars on hand and rotate them into your beauty regimen whenever you need to purify and freshen your skin.

Shopping List

- 1½ cups white glycerin soap base
- 4 drops cedarwood essential oil
- 2 tablespoons activated charcoal
- Three 3"-square soap molds
- Rubbing alcohol in small spray bottle
- Microwave-safe container
- Wooden stir stick

Calming Cedarwood

Cedarwood essential oil is a perfect ingredient to combine with charcoal. After the charcoal detoxifies skin, cedarwood acts as a natural antibacterial, helping to prevent bacteria from penetrating the skin again. Cedarwood can also soothe dry or itchy skin, and its scent has a calming effect that can promote relaxation.

MAKE IT! • CHARCOAL CLEANSING BAR

1 Melt the glycerin soap base.

2 Add the essential oil and activated charcoal. Stir well and pour into the molds.

3 Lightly spray the surface of the soap with the rubbing alcohol to remove bubbles. Let the soap set until firm and remove from the molds.

Charcoal Cleanse

Activated charcoal draws impurities from the skin, helping to make pores less visible. It can help to treat acne and balance oily skin by removing excess oil. Charcoal can also help to soothe and heal skin irritations.

Use tissue paper or gift wrap to wrap each soap. Take two gift tags and glue the ends together. Fold the tags around the soap and secure with twine and decorative ribbon. Use stamps to label the front of each soap.

Mini Soap Flowers

MAKES 10 MINI SOAPS

Infused with rose essential oil and rose petals, these mini soaps are filled with healing and calming benefits, all in an adorable little package. Milk and rose are a powerful combination for your skin. Both are soothing and help to repair the skin and prevent wrinkles, leaving you with a beautiful complexion. Use this soap at the end of a long day when you could use a little extra pampering. Make a large batch and store them in a glass container so they're always on hand when you need them.

Shopping List

- 1½ cups goat's milk suspension formula soap base
- 6 drops rose essential oil
- 6 drops pink soap coloring
- Dried rose petals
- 10-flower ice cube tray (mine is 11" x 5")
- Rubbing alcohol in small spray bottle
- Microwave-safe container
- Wooden stir stick

Healing Rose

Rose is credited with many healing properties. The scent of rose essential oil is said to be calming and soothing, while rose petals offer many skin-healing benefits. Rose itself can help repair damaged skin and tighten it to reduce wrinkles, but it also increases skin's permeability, helping your skin absorb other beneficial ingredients you may include in your soap recipes.

MAKE IT! • MINI SOAP FLOWERS

1 Melt the goat's milk soap base.

2 Add the essential oil and soap coloring and stir well.

3 Add 1–2 spoonfuls of rose petals and mix well. Pour into the ice cube tray.

4 Lightly spray the surface of the soap with the rubbing alcohol to remove bubbles. Let the soap set until firm and remove from the mold.

Fill a lidded jar with these mini soap flowers. For a decorative touch, try adding ribbon, attaching a label with twine, or creating a chalkboard label with a chalkboard sticker and a white paint pen.

Lime & Coconut Soap

MAKES 3 BARS

The combination of lime and coconut makes this soap smell like a beach vacation. And with the coconut milk base, this soap has all the properties to help you pamper your skin like you're on vacation too. Coconut milk soap is known for its ability to deep-clean skin without drying it out, so you can get refreshingly clean while keeping your skin smooth and moisturized. The chopped coconut adds just a bit of exfoliating texture to gently polish your skin, making it soft and silky.

Shopping List

- 2½ cups coconut milk soap base
- 4–6 drops green soap coloring
- 10 drops lime essential oil
- ½ cup finely chopped organic coconut
- 6-rectangle soap mold (mine is 9" x 8")
- Rubbing alcohol in small spray bottle
- Microwave-safe container
- Wooden stir stick

Uplifting Lime

Lime essential oil is known to positively affect your mood and promote emotional balance. It may even help to spark your creativity. Applied to the skin, as in this soap, lime essential oil can also help to deter insects.

MAKE IT! • LIME & COCONUT SOAP

1 Prepare the mold by adding a layer of chopped coconut to the bottom of each space.

2 Melt the coconut milk soap base. Add the soap coloring and essential oil. Stir well and pour into the mold.

3 Lightly spray the surface of the soap with the rubbing alcohol to remove bubbles. Let the soap set until firm and remove from the mold.

Moisturizing Coconut

Coconut milk soap has the unique ability to deeply cleanse the skin by removing impurities without dehydrating it. Coconut milk's fatty acids are incredibly moisturizing, helping to make skin soft and supple. Enriched with vitamins and antioxidants, coconut milk can also help to prevent wrinkles.

Package each soap in a decorative envelope or box or wrap them in decorative paper. Wrap each package with string. For a decorative touch, add a circular label and a paper flower.

Marbled Lemon Bliss Soap on a Rope

MAKES 1 BAR

The twine, marbled color, and wavy texture of this soap produces a handmade look that's perfect for gift-giving. The shea butter base is a wonderful way to moisturize your skin, while the invigorating lemon scent will lift your mood and hint at the beautiful days of summer. You can combine this recipe with any citrus essential oil like orange, grapefruit, lime, or even tangerine. Have fun experimenting to discover your favorite, or make some of each to have a range of options available for you and your guests.

Shopping List

- 1 cup shea butter soap base
- 5–6 drops lemon essential oil
- 3–4 drops yellow soap coloring
- ½ teaspoon poppy seeds (optional)
- 2¾" x 3½" rectangular soap mold
- Rubbing alcohol in small spray bottle
- Microwave-safe container
- Wooden stir stick
- Twine
- Wavy soap slicer

> ***Lemon Zest***
> Citrus fruits are loaded with beneficial antioxidants and Vitamin C. Lemon essential oil is particularly known for its ability to help cleanse toxins from the body, purify and nourish skin, and revitalize your mood.

MAKE IT! • MARBLED LEMON BLISS SOAP ON A ROPE

1 Prepare the mold by making a tiny cut in the top of the rectangle for the twine. Cut a short length of twine and push it through the cut you made, forming a loop on the outside of the mold with the tails of the twine on the inside of the mold.

2 Melt the shea butter soap base. Add the lemon essential oil and stir. If desired, also add the poppy seeds and stir. Pour a small amount of the melted soap into a second container and stir in the soap coloring. You may need to reheat it for 15–20 seconds.

3 Pour some of the white soap into the mold and then add a little of the yellow soap. Repeat, alternating colors until the mold is full. The colors should mix as you pour, or you can use a spoon to swirl them slightly.

4 Lightly spray the surface of the soap with the rubbing alcohol to remove bubbles. Let the soap set until firm and remove from the mold.

5 Use a wavy soap slicer to cut a small slice off the front and back of the soap, creating a handmade finish. You'll also be able to see the marbled colors better.

Package each soap in an envelope or paper bag and fold over the top to close it. Make a label, and use baker's twine to attach it to the soap and secure the top of the bag. Yellow baker's twine is the perfect match for this yellow soap recipe.

Coffee Latte Soap

MAKES 3 BARS

If you're a coffee-lover, this soap is for you. The amazing scent of vanilla and coffee combined with the skin-nourishing ingredients and rich lather of the glycerin soap base make a wonderful way to enhance your morning shower. The coffee adds a delightful texture to revitalize and exfoliate skin. Combine this soap with your favorite moisturizer to start off the day with soft, glowing skin.

Shopping List

- 1½ cups white glycerin soap base
- 2 tablespoons ground coffee
- 6 drops vanilla fragrance
- Three 3"-square soap molds
- Rubbing alcohol in small spray bottle
- Microwave-safe container
- Wooden stir stick

Coffee Kickstart

Just like a coffee beverage helps wake you up in the morning, the coffee in this soap helps stimulate your skin. The antioxidants found in coffee can also help soothe skin.

1 Melt the glycerin soap base.

2 Add the coffee and vanilla fragrance. Mix well and pour into the molds.

3 Lightly spray the surface of the soap with the rubbing alcohol to remove bubbles. Let the soap set until firm and remove from the molds.

Sensational Scents

I love pairing this recipe with vanilla fragrance, but there are lots of scents you could use. Try chocolate, caramel, hazelnut, or cinnamon. Use your creativity and experiment with a few different options until you find your favorite!

Crumple a piece of butcher paper or a brown paper bag to give it some texture. Wrap a strip of paper around each soap and secure with tape. Tie twine over the paper.

Loofah Sponge Soap

MAKES 2 SOAPS

This recipe gives you soap and a sponge all in one! If your sponge is small enough, you can make these soaps using a silicone cupcake pan as your mold. To mix it up, trying using a glycerin soap base and substitute the green soap coloring for your favorite color. These soaps make wonderful gifts. Try packaging them with other homemade bath treats like scrubs or lotions for a spa day gift basket.

Shopping List

- 1½ cups shea butter soap base
- 6–7 drops tea tree essential oil
- 3 drops green soap coloring
- 3"-diameter loofah sponge
- Two 3"-diameter paper ice cream cups
- Rubbing alcohol in small spray bottle
- Microwave-safe container
- Wooden stir stick
- Sharp knife

Tea Tree Treat

Tea tree essential oil is known as a powerful antibacterial, making it an excellent choice for a soap ingredient. A natural anti-inflammatory, it can also help to soothe irritated or inflamed skin.

MAKE IT! • LOOFAH SPONGE SOAP

1 Cut 2 slices from the loofah sponge with a sharp knife. Place each sponge slice in a paper cup mold.

2 Melt the shea butter soap base. Add the essential oil and soap coloring and mix well.

3 Pour the soap into the cups. Lightly spray the surface of the soap with the rubbing alcohol to remove bubbles.

4 Let the soap set until firm and remove from the cups by tearing away the paper.

Create labels for the soap. Place each soap in a decorative dish. Use twine or decorative string to secure the soap in place and tie on the label.

Classic Lavender Soap

MAKES 2 BARS

This beautifully simple soap takes advantage of all the benefits of lavender. The calming and relaxing scent makes it perfect for use in the evening to wind down after a long day and promote a restful night's sleep. The shea butter will help lock in moisture overnight so you can wake up to smooth, soft skin. Package a few of these soaps together and give them to a friend or family member who could use some well-deserved relaxation.

Shopping List

- 1½ cups shea butter suspension formula soap base
- 1–2 teaspoons dried lavender
- 5–7 drops lavender essential oil
- Two 3"-diameter basic round soap molds
- Rubbing alcohol in small spray bottle
- Microwave-safe container
- Wooden stir stick

Soothing Lavender

Lavender essential oil is known to relieve stress and anxiety, while the soothing scent aids in sleep. It can also help to relieve pain and enhance circulation, so try applying this lavender-infused soap to stiff or sore muscles.

MAKE IT! • CLASSIC LAVENDER SOAP

1 Melt the shea butter soap base.

2 Add the dried lavender and essential oil. Mix well and pour into the molds. Lightly spray the surface of the soap with the rubbing alcohol to remove bubbles.

3 Let the soap set until firm and remove from the molds.

Smoothing Shea Butter

Chock full of vitamins and fatty acids, shea butter is a wonderful way to moisturize skin and is particularly soothing after sun exposure. Shea butter supports skin's natural collagen production, helping to strengthen and smooth skin.

Use stamps to create decorative labels for the soap. Wrap each soap in a coffee filter and secure it in place with the label, using glue if necessary..

Meet Kimberly Layton

Driven by a lifelong love of making things, Kimberly Layton took her crafting to a whole new level in 2008. She is now a full-time professional blogger, craft book author, and creative business coach.

Kimberly blogs about Etsy business and all manner of DIY craft things at EverythingEtsy.com, and shares a more personal side along with creative business ideas at KimberlyLayton.com. She also can be found as @EverythingEtsy on Instagram, Facebook, Pinterest, and Twitter.

Kimberly likes dabbling in all kinds of crafts, but creating simple handmade gifts tops them all. She started blogging to promote her first Etsy shop full of sweet little felt creations. From there, it's grown to coaching and social media training for creative businesses.

Traveling is Kimberly's other favorite pastime. She and her family have visited all of the lower 48 states and have traveled as far away as the Great Barrier Reef! Just mention the word "go" and Kimberly and family are there!

Made in U.S.A.

Library of Congress Control Number: 2018945349

We have made every effort to ensure that these instructions are accurate and complete. We cannot, however, be responsible for human error, typographical mistakes, or variations in individual work.

Production Team: Technical Editors – Lisa Lancaster and Katie Weeber; Senior Graphic Designer – Lora Puls; Graphic Designer – Ashley Millhouse; Photo Stylist – Lori Wenger; Photographer – Jason Masters.

This book cannot guarantee that creating the projects in this book is safe for everyone. For this reason, this book is sold without warranties or guarantees of any kind, expressed or implied, and the publisher and the author disclaim any liability for any injuries, losses, or damages caused in any way by the content of this book or the reader's use of the materials needed to complete the projects presented here. The publisher and the author urge all readers to thoroughly review each project and to understand the use of all materials before beginning any project.